Jim Gray
Mark Monday
Gary Stubblefield

Maritime TERROR

Protecting Yourself, Your Vessel, and Your Crew against Piracy

Paladin Press · Boulder, Colorado

Maritime Terror:
  Protecting Yourself, Your Vessel, and Your Crew against Piracy

by Jim Gray, Mark Monday, and Gary Stubblefield

Copyright © 1999 by Vantage Systems, Inc.

ISBN 1-58160-015-1
Printed in the United States of America

Published by Sycamore Island Books, a division of
Paladin Enterprises, Inc., P.O. Box 1307,
Boulder, Colorado 80306, USA.
(303) 443-7250

Direct inquiries and/or orders to the above address.

Table of Contents

This book is dedicated to all seafarers who risk their lives and fortunes on the waters of the world—today, yesterday, and tomorrow.

We owe special thanks to our mentors on the bridge and at the keyboard:

Capt. Frank Gillies, J. Bowyer Bell, Bob Early, and Hans Halberstadt. Special thanks are owed our editor, Karen Pochert, who guided us through the treacherous waters of publishing like a pilot at the bar.

To them all, we wish fair winds and calm seas.

Preface

Travel by water is becoming increasingly problematic. The recent boarding of and theft from a "mega-yacht" off the French coast, a shooting attack against a yacht off Somalia, the 1998 hijacking of an oil tanker to China, the increase in piracy in the Asian region, and an explosive stowaway problem in several refugee-ridden regions of the world are all examples of the difficulties all modern seamen—whether ship captains or yacht owners—face. Too often they face these problems alone and unprepared.

Pirates are a worldwide problem, but they are not the only problem. Their cousins in crime, maritime terrorists, are taking aim at ships, too. A relatively new phenomenon—firing at ships in channels—has gained notoriety and was rather successful in Egypt, where the rebel group Gama'a conducted a waterside ambush campaign against Nile cruisers, causing casualties among the passengers and crew of the tourist boats. While the practice of ambushing tourist cruisers has not become widespread, the genie is out of the bottle. The tactic is likely to produce copycat attacks, or, of even greater concern, improved attack techniques that are likely to be used against yachts and other shipping.

This manual is designed to help the modern sailor make sure the adventure of yachting doesn't turn into catastrophe. The book is not a magic shield that will turn bullets. It will not blast would-be marauders off a gangplank. However, the information here is one piece of a comprehensive program that should include formulating, provisioning, training, and testing of a yacht security plan to ensure that you are as safe as you can be in a world that is itself uncertain and unsafe.

The Increasing Threat of Piracy

Piracy—including boardings, attempted boardings, hijackings, detentions, and robberies at port or anchorage—remains a hidden but very real problem in many areas of the world.

The crews of some hijacked ships have been marooned or even thrown overboard by the sea raiders. Some victims are found. Other crews simply disappear. In addition to the cost in lives, the price of piracy is high in economic terms. Estimates of the monetary cost of piracy and maritime fraud range as high as $16 billion a year. While the number of reported attacks is high—and has been growing—the actual count appears to be even higher. Many ship's masters discourage seamen from reporting pirate attacks, apparently because of the delays that the vessel may encounter as reporting formalities are completed.

Some pirates are simple local fishermen who supplement their income by occasional piratical attacks. They hit weak-appearing targets of opportunity. This happened many times to those unfortunate targets known as "boat people" who escaped the bonds of the newly formed Vietnamese government only to have their vessels boarded by fishermen and others. These unfortunates lost their few worldly possessions—and sometimes their lives.

On the other end of the scale are the trained terrorists who want to hold you and your guests as hostages—not to mention the expensive vessels—in order to make a political statement.

Pirates are attacking everything from container ships and tankers to ferries and yachts. Even passenger liners are not immune.

For instance, in 1985 a team of Palestinian terrorists answering to Abul Abbas hijacked the *Achille Lauro*. While Abbas claims his gunmen only intended to use the cruise liner as a means to slip into Israel, not commandeer the vessel, that was not how things worked out. His hijackers didn't face armed troops; instead they shot an elderly, infirm American in his wheelchair and tossed the body overboard. The seagoing terrorists held more than 300 passengers hostage off Port Said, Egypt, for two days before surrendering to Egyptian authorities.

Egypt, unwilling to deal with the pirates, immediately shipped Abbas and his men off to Tunisia, where he was headquartered. Incensed, the U.S. government sent navy fighters after the plane the hijackers were in and forced the flight down in Sicily.

Italy, in yet another demonstration of the continued unwillingness of even Western governments to deal with piratical killers, freed Abbas. The Italians allowed him to flee to Yugoslavia before the American arrest warrant for

Boat people escaping from Indochina/Vietnam typically fell prey to pirates in vessels such as the one shown here. This type of pirate vessel is still commonly used in attacks against fishermen and boaters in these Third World areas.

Modern-day pirates often approach in swarms of small, high-speed boats and execute quick and violent attacks.

piracy and hostage taking could be served. This unwilling-ness or inability of government to cope with the piracy problem—leaving the troubles on the doorstep of every cap-tain and seaman—is a worldwide phenomenon.

Commercial craft are not the only targets; yachts are proving to be particularly attractive to seagoing terrorists because the crews are small and are seldom prepared to defend themselves. Most important of all considerations, yachts—ton for ton—usually have exceptionally large amounts of cash, salable equipment, and things of value aboard. As an example, in August 1996 four pirates using a small pedal-powered dinghy and wielding a handgun attacked a British yacht and robbed six French passengers of cash and jewelry worth thousands of dollars. Italian media said the yacht *Renalo* was moored off the coast of Calabria in the toe of the boot of Italy, having arrived at the seaside town of Scilla just hours before the bandits struck. One report said the pirates had asked a lifeguard at the beach if they could rent his *pedalo*, or pedal-powered dinghy, threatening him with a pistol when he refused. Then, paddling toward the *Renalo*, which was moored only hundreds of yards from the shore, the robbers drew along-side the 272-foot (34-meter) yacht. They boarded it and tied up the six crew and six passengers. Police said the pirates stole the equivalent of $2,600 in currency and pocketed jewelry worth thousands of dollars. The thieves then made off in an inflatable powerboat that had been stolen earlier and was brought to the scene of the crime by an accomplice.

The use of such small, high-speed craft has become more prevalent, and boardings have increased worldwide.

There is an accompanying and disturbing trend toward the use of firearms and physical violence—often gratuitous violence—even after a ship has been boarded and the pirates are in firm control. Modern-day pirates are bolder in their actions and use heavier weapons than they did only a decade ago. They no longer content themselves with small arms and knives; they are not just indulging in petty thefts. In some documented attacks they used machine guns and grenades to hijack vessels and cargoes. In at least one case— in Philippine waters—they dimpled the hull of a tanker with rocket fire.

Pirates' proclivity for individual violence seems to be growing as well. "There is no doubt that attacks on vessels have become more audacious, more violent and an issue of serious concern to shipping and seamen," stated the Regional Piracy Center (RPC) of the International Maritime Bureau (IMB) in its 1996 annual report. The comment is growing more familiar each year. The human body count has been going up as steadily as a thermometer in the Sahara. The authoritative Regional Piracy Center of the International Maritime Bureau (IMB) said that in 1997 pirates killed at least 51 seamen, compared with 26 in the previous year. More than 400 crew members were taken hostage during 1997, compared with 194 the year before. Seagoing terrorists fired on ships 26 times in that period, up from just 6 times in 1996.

The violence continues. In early May 1998 pirates opened fire on the Cypriot-flagged *Leros Star* in the Gulf of Aden, wounding a Polish crew member. Later that month pirates attacked a Lithuanian merchant vessel in the Indian Ocean, seriously wounding one of the officers on board.

The attackers boarded the *Algirdas* while the ship was en route from Calcutta to Singapore. The ship was reportedly about 40 miles off the Thai island of Pukhet when a smaller vessel carrying about 25 pirates attacked. Ten armed men boarded the ship and some fired on the crew, shooting the second-in-command through the throat, media reports said. The pirates reportedly tied the crew to the ship's rail and destroyed the ship's radio prior to looting the vessel of personal belongings and any other valuables they could find. One of the crew eventually managed to free himself after the pirates left and sent out a report on a portable telephone.

According to IMB officials, "Modern piracy is violent, bloody and ruthless. It is made all the more fearsome because its victims know they are alone and defenseless."

The attackers are even organizing. Pirates sometimes group their resources, forming powerful syndicates. In the most plotted-out plans a pirate syndicate will seize a ship, fraudulently reflag it, and sell it off to an unsuspecting buyer (or at least one who will look the other way if he suspects anything).

In both Sri Lanka and the Philippines, paramilitary forces of rebels have hijacked large boats as part of their operations. In Sri Lanka the rebel naval force—the Sea Tigers, as the guerrillas are known—operates in "wolf packs" of high-speed fiberglass dinghies. The rebel boats are powered by multiple outboard motors capable of reaching speeds of 30 knots. The craft have mounted guns and rocket launchers. Each boat usually carries five or six guerrilla fighters, and, en masse, they are formidable opponents. Even aircraft and government patrol craft have a hard time operating against the Sea Tigers when they move as a large force.

In addition, several mid-Eastern terrorist groups—backed by what many consider to be an outlaw government—have their own naval forces capable of operating against civilian shipping or undefended pleasure craft.

Vessels that are sailing without the proper equipment and are crewed by people who are untrained in dealing with the unique problems posed by piracy are attractive targets to this modern generation of seaborne terrorists.

Another type of seagoing incident that, while not traditionally thought of as piracy, can be costly to the vessel owner or corporation is when one or more individuals sneaks aboard the ship or yacht as it sails away from the port. Once aboard, the stowaway becomes the responsibility of the vessel and its owner. The costs to return the stowaway, in terms of money, time, and legal costs, can be significant in many countries. Officials at the next port of call can discover the stowaway and force the vessel to bear all costs of prosecution as well as the expenses of getting the stowaway back to the earlier port. Shipmasters and owners may even face legal actions for allowing the incident to have occurred. Given the worldwide refugee problem and the number of nations where residents are desperate to flee, stowaways have become a problem of mega-proportions. In some areas, such as along the Red Sea, this has become a serious situation for shipping. In Djibouti, the local government reportedly assists and encourages stowaways by telling refugees how to get aboard vessels.

Clearly, the crews of high-value targets need to be trained how to protect themselves and their vessels against a broad range of threats—from stowaways to political terrorists. Captains need to be well versed in—and willing to employ—techniques that will discourage intruders from boarding in the first place: prevention, if you will. And if attacked, the captain and crew need to be capable of repelling the marauders with minimal casualties to themselves and minimal damage to the vessel.

A quality trained crew and captain are simply good investments. In the case of a mega-yacht, the owner spends a large amount of money for the initial outlay of the yacht as well as a significant amount on an ongoing basis for everything from hull insurance to a well-stocked larder and fine-wine list to bottom scraping, fuel, and salaries for the seamen. For very little additional outlay, the owner can

have his crew trained and his vessel outfitted to best prevent or deter acts of piracy. A well-versed and alert yacht
crew can hold off attackers under all but the most difficult
and dangerous of situations.

Chapter One

Evaluating the Threat:

An Overview of Piracy

N

W E

S

Pirates often conjure up the vision of colorful 17th-century swashbucklers battling oppressive naval establishments and inhuman conditions at sea. Modern piracy is anything but romantic. The modern pirate may be a thief, mugger, rapist, murderer, terrorist, or any combination of these terrible types. Modern pirates are not people you want aboard your vessel or in control of your life.

THREE SCENARIOS OF MODERN PIRACY

Today there are three common piracy scenarios.

In the simplest version the pirates simply rob the crew and then depart over the side. Most often this occurs when the victim vessel is at anchor. The *Renalo* incident is typical of this type of attack. Some consider this penny-ante crime, but attacks like this can easily result in death or injury for owners, passengers, and crew of yachts.

In the second type of piracy the thieves target the entire cargo, or the people, aboard the victimized vessel rather than looking for a few expensive possessions and pocket change. Cargo can be resold, quite often on the black market, and people can be ransomed. In some cases the craft—if it is not unique or highly unusual—can be repainted, altered, and renamed. The vessel can then be sold to an unsuspecting buyer in some port far from the scene of the pirate attack. In these types of cases the pirates generally try to leave no witnesses to the takeover.

The third type of pirate attack is one in which pirates buy or take over a vessel, reflag it, and then run a "phantom ship" that hijacks the cargo of anyone foolish enough to consign goods to it. The pirates may also use the vessel to haul illicit drugs or other contraband. The phantom ship trick involves sophisticated gangs who are able to steal at least $200 million per year worth of cargo. Many of the ships are then flagged in Honduras and Panama and take cargo that is easily disposed of but not easily traced, such as timber, metals, and minerals. Although the "phantom ship" scenario is not one faced by yacht owners, its significance to yacht owners lies in pointing out that masters and crew must be prepared to deal with people who are capable of thinking. A defense against sheer thuggery is not enough.

LOCATIONS AND TYPES OF PIRACY

Pirates arrive in all types of vessels and strike even in places not noted for piracy.

While piracy is endemic and pervasive in some areas, attacks can happen almost anywhere. Regions without a history of attacks can suddenly find themselves scupper-deep in seaborne raiders.

A vessel of this type, frequently seen around Indonesia and the Philippines, may be innocent, or it may be involved in acts of piracy.

Though Peru is not considered one of the traditional hotbeds of piracy, in late June 1998 pirates attacked a score of Peruvian fishing vessels. The raiders would shoot in from Ecuadorian waters to prey on the fishing vessels on speedboats. The ski-masked and heavily armed pirates boarded their hapless, helpless targets to steal everything of value, including electronics and the fish catches. At least a dozen fishermen were reported injured in the series of boardings.

Iranian waters aren't listed among the most dangerous either, but in Tehran, in July 1998, the Iranian police reportedly broke up a network of pirates. The sea-thieves robbed and killed crews of commercial craft operating in the Gulf. Using speedboats, the pirates reportedly intercepted vessels moving cargoes of cigarettes between Iranian ports and other Gulf harbors, killing 11 people during their depredations.

European waters are not noted for pirates, but recall the August 1996 attack a British yacht *Renalo* off the Calabrian coast. Four pirates using a small pedal-powered dinghy and wielding a handgun robbed six French passengers of cash and jewelry worth thousands of dollars. They were lucky.

Occasionally yacht attacks have an even sadder ending. The yacht *Carenia* was riding quietly at anchor in a Corfu cove on September 27, 1996, when four attackers in a speedboat pulled alongside about midnight. The owner of the yacht, Keith Hedley, woke up and attempted to foil the marine marauders with a shotgun blast. His too-little-too-late effort came to naught; Hedley and three friends were held at gunpoint while the pirates ransacked the yacht for valuables. The shotgun blast, though it didn't hold off the pirates, brought police pelting out. They drew up while the pirates were still aboard the *Carenia*. Hedley was fatally wounded during the ensuing gunfight between police and pirates. And the pirates escaped. Pirates very often escape. For most, piracy is a low-risk, high-paying job when compared with other lines of work they qualify for.

The world leaders in pirate attacks in 1996 were the same six countries that have historically shared the distinction.

The six—the sites of more than half of the recorded attacks—were Indonesia, Thailand, Brazil, the Philippines, Sri Lanka, and India.

Modern pirates, as in the past, come in three types. There is the purely criminal variety, the semi-official military variety, and the terrorist type, who may have had military special operations training.

The terrorist type may be the most difficult to deal with, but all three types need to be reckoned with in many areas of the world.

The location of the pirate attack—the area of the world and the type of waterway where the attack occurs—often dictates the type of pirate that a captain and crew are likely to encounter and the level of violence they can expect.

Pirate attacks happen in the following areas:

- The open ocean
- Restricted waterways
- Anchorages
- Pierside

Open ocean attacks on large vessels while under way usually require a trained team to assure success. Such attacks are among the most serious. Often the target of such open ocean attacks will be hijacked and sailed off to some port or rendezvous where the cargo will be removed and the ship may be renamed and reflagged. Crews of vessels targeted in open ocean attacks are often killed or forced to abandon ship in precarious circumstances. After all, pirates today—like those of old—prefer to leave no witnesses. Open ocean attacks on small defenseless craft, like the attacks perpetrated against the "boat people" of Vietnam, may be carried out by relative amateurs. Historically, even here, the attackers have shown a preference to leave no tattletales alive.

Canal channels, rivers, straits, harbors, or any narrow waterways are often prime targeting areas for the second

Another example of what a typical pirate's vessel might look like.

type of pirate attack. The targeted vessels are physically forced through narrow channels that restrict both their maneuverability and the options they have to avoid pirates. The Strait of Malacca, between the island-studded coastlines of Malaysia and Indonesia, is one of the best known locations for narrow-waterway attacks. Here, once the pirates have attacked their victims they can easily disappear into well over 10,000 island lairs. There are examples of this narrow waterway type of attack even in the United States, where small ships and crews navigating the rivers and bayous between Florida and Louisiana are victimized. The American pirates sometimes use small craft, but in many cases will even attack moored boats from land. A land-launched attack gives them speed, mobility, and ease of escape over the well-developed road system.

Moorages and anchorages can become prime pirate areas. Even vessels that are rafted up and moored alongside one another are not immune. Pirates find the approach is easy in an anchorage. Sitting snugly in what they consider a safe harbor or roadstead, ships' crews are generally unsuspecting. There are small craft around all the time. The close approach of a boat may go mentally unnoted, even if the craft is noticed. At night the pirates may use stealth and darkness as a cover and drift down on the target from a screen of vessels in the vicinity. Once the pirates have successfully attacked the target they disappear into the maze of the surrounding vessels or return to a nearby port facility where they remove the spoils and easily dispose of them on the black or gray market. Vessels will seldom be hijacked in this type of pirate attack—getting the ship under way is usually beyond the pirates' capabilities. These attackers usually want things they can carry away, not the ship and cargo.

Pierside attacks are less common. In most instances the thefts will be relatively petty. Violence is always a possibility; however, the pierside pirate is usually more interested in filching a few items or dollars that he can carry away than he is in physical violence. Pierside attackers don't necessarily use a vessel to approach the target. They can swim or walk to the victim vessel. Once they have their booty—almost always man-portable—they can walk down the gangway and disappear into the maze of shoreline structures. This is territory they are familiar with, among a population they know, in a place where they can fence the stolen valuables or spend the money.

TROUBLE SPOTS

While some experts insist that "piracy moves around," the statement is misleading. Piracy-plagued areas are piracy-plagued areas.

Pirates may simply be more or less active—or their victims may be more or less willing to make reports—at any given time. While a particular area may rank number one in a given year and number three the following year, the same areas are generally on the list of the top five over a period of years. Only their relative position on the chart will change.

Temporary changes may be due to the pressures put on the pirates by local navies, maritime law enforcement agencies, and, sometimes, by the police ashore. While international concerns will often put pressure on navies or nations to make the problem "disappear" for a short while, the pirates and the problem inevitably return.

Any place that is rarely patrolled, or is patrolled by less-than-professional forces, is prone to piracy. Where there are restricting channels or shoals, or where the vessels in the waterway can be expected to hold valuable cargo, piracy flourishes. By the same token, the outer anchorages and even piers of many busy, crowded ports are prime areas for piratical boardings and robberies. These are places where the ships cannot move and the emergency response time is poor.

The South China Sea and adjacent waters, as well as the Indonesian waters, have been some of the most active areas for pirates. China, Hong Kong and Macau, Thailand, and India are also among the areas considered most dangerous. So are some areas off Central and South America, as well as off the coast of Africa. The Caribbean can be a particularly troublesome area for U.S. vessels.

Southeast Asia-Chinese Waters

The Hong Kong-Luzon-Hainan triangle has traditionally been a favorite hunting ground for pirates, but the danger area is even larger than that. Virtually the entire South China Sea and adjacent waterways can be considered dangerous. Although the number of attacks in this area may fluctuate, there is always reason for concern here. There is a serious problem of ship hijackings associated with attacks in the Philippines and adjacent waters. Significantly, many of the ships hijacked throughout this area of the world have reportedly been taken to Chinese ports, where the cargoes have been removed. Scuttlebutt among the shipping community suggests North Korea is the final port of call for the remainder of the untraced shipping.

Piracy in Philippine waters has a high probability of being exceptionally violent. There is a tradition of violence among Philippine pirates. They often use heavy weapons. They will kill at the slightest provocation—or even no provocation at all.

On January 9, 1998, four fishermen were kidnapped and killed by pirates off Basilan Island in the Philippines. The bodies of the four, bearing multiple machete-wounds, were found floating off the shore of Basilan two days after their boat was seized while fishing in the area.

On October 17, 1997, pirates struck a fatal blow near Manila. A Chinese ship's engineer was killed when four pirates attacked his vessel soon after it arrived in the Philippine capital from Hong Kong. The cargo ship, MV *Yi He*, carrying a crew of 30, arrived in Manila Bay before dawn and was anchored off the city's harbor when four pirates boarded the vessel from a motorboat. The ship's engineer tried to resist the pirates but was shot and fatally wounded before the arrival of coastguardsmen.

In another, all-too-typical attack in the southern Philippines, the 10-man crew of the fishing vessel *Normina* was working when a pair of speedboats—two men in each boat—raced up. Hauling out automatic weapons, the quartet slew nine of the unarmed crewmen in less than a minute. Only one of the men—wounded—was able to leap overboard at the time of the attack, on February 26, 1996. He eventually was rescued, but the *Normina* has not been seen since.

There is also an insurgent dimension to the piracy problem in the southern Philippines. Muslim rebels attack boats to demonstrate their control of the area while simultaneously looting supplies and money to buy more and better arms. In some cases even ferryboats have fallen prey to these rebel pirates, with deadly results. On February 23, 1997, the fundamentalist pirates hijacked a ferry in the Philippines, killing three passengers and robbing 50 others.

Some of the piracy in and around Chinese waters has a quasi-official quality. There is an appearance—at the very least—of official connivance. The suspicions of official complicity have been so widespread and persistent that the Chinese government has been forced to formally deny reports that official government agencies carry out pirate attacks! The concern about the collaboration, or direct involvement, of Chinese officials in the piracy off the Chinese coast is seconded by a recent IMB report that says, "Vessels continue to report that they have been shad-owed, boarded, or hijacked by Chinese customs launches or vessels that resemble them." The IMB specifically pointed out the case of the *Anna Sierra*.

About 30 pirates swarmed over the Cypriot-registered *Anna Sierra* with its $4 million cargo of sugar, as the ves-sel cruised in the Gulf of Thailand on September 13, 1995. After the pirates gained control of the ship about half of them left. They repainted and renamed the vessel, then tossed the crew into the sea in two groups, alongside makeshift life rafts, leaving them without water or food. The pirates sailed the renamed ship off to China; the crew was rescued after two days at sea by Vietnamese-crewed fishing boats.

The renamed vessel was spotted in a Chinese harbor, and the local authorities boarded the ship. They restricted the pirates but did not jail them. Chinese authorities even-tually freed the piratical crew—reportedly identified in their passports as entrepreneurs—and years later auctioned off the cargo.

There was considerable cause for suspicion, and much talk in shipping circles, that the Chinese government offi-cially sanctioned this piratical act or that the perpetrators enjoyed the protection of Chinese officials.

The suspicions of collusion became stronger in 1998. On April 17, 1998, the *Petro Ranger* was hijacked while bound to Vietnam from Singapore with a $1.5 million cargo of diesel fuel and kerosene. About a dozen Indonesian pirates used ropes to board the vessel and overpowered the ship's 21 crewmen. A day later the tanker—with a new name, a new flag, and a new funnel color, sailed away. The vessel was found in Haikou, China, on April 26, as the cargo was being siphoned into a Chinese-registered tanker. But port authorities backed and filled. In a reprise of the *Anna Sierra* case they showed great reluctance to do any-thing about the matter—including identifying the vessel as the hijacked ship.

Small ships are not immune to dangers in the region either. On May Day of 1996, pistol-armed pirates drew up alongside a fishing trawler in Chinese waters and rushed aboard. They ransacked the trawler, which was registered in Hong Kong. They stole thousands of dollars in cash and jewelry—as well as identity cards—before fleeing. The gunmen wounded the craft's owner when he resisted the attack.

There are unproved—though not inconsistent—reports that some of the ships hijacked in this area have been taken to the Stalinist rogue state of North Korea. There the hijackers reportedly have sanctuary—and the government gets the goodies, according to the story making the rounds in shipping circles.

Indonesia-Malacca Straits

Indonesia has seen steady growth in piracy. Much of the reported piracy in Indonesian waters is directed at

Vessels like this one can easily fall prey to pirates who steal the cargo and then repaint and reregister the freighter in order to make the venture even more profitable.

anchored ships, although there has been a string of often-unsolved commando-style tanker attacks that should send any seafarer in the region to his worry beads.

The *Petro Ranger* strike was just one of a string. She was the third tanker carrying fuel to be hit by pirates since the previous November 17. The first was *Atlanta 15*, which was hijacked in Riau Straits, Indonesia. On January 11, pirates operating near Aur Island in East Malaysia boarded the *Tioman 1*. In all the incidents an unidentified tanker came alongside to siphon the fuel.

Tankers are a prize for pirates, and they have been disappearing with an alarming frequency in the region. On November 11, 1996, pirates boarded a Malaysian-flagged tanker near Singapore and held the crew. A day later the pirates dropped most of the crew into a life raft and sailed away after doing a quick renaming and repaint job.

When tankers aren't available, there are other prizes. More recently, pirates wounded a crewman while trying to plunder a Vietnamese ship carrying 7,100 tons of rice. The attack occurred near Cilegon, Indonesia, on the night of March 12, 1998. Five or more pirates reportedly boarded the MV *Nam Dhiem* that night. They shot a crewman who confronted them in the stomach, then fled in the speedboat they arrived in.

Indonesia's economic problems—soaring unemployment and rapid inflation—will likely contribute to the regional piracy problems. The economic incentive for piracy has skyrocketed while Indonesia's maritime protection forces face financial difficulties in an era of dwindling resources. The country of about 13,000 islands extends for 3,000 miles along the key sea lanes used by many of the ships traveling between Asia and Europe. The Straits of Malacca seriously restrict speed and maneuverability. There is plenty of opportunity for both organized and amateur sea thieves to make a killing. The cargoes aboard a vessel may be worth hundreds of millions of dollars. With every financial tumble and stumble in the area, the equation gets weighted more heavily in favor of piracy.

Attacks can happen quickly in the Malacca Straits— along the Malaysia-Indonesia-Thailand sea corridor. For instance, on April 21, 1996, pirates armed with knives boarded a German-flagged container ship off Bangkok. After taking control of the vessel, they stole a quantity of paint and escaped. The attack took only 10 minutes.

Occasionally the pirates don't get away. In an unusual event on October 27, 1997, Thai navy officials reported arresting 11 pirates who had commandeered a tanker. The *Oriental City* had been seized on the high seas about 200 nautical miles southeast of a province bordering Malaysia, according to the military. The tanker was carrying about one million liters of diesel fuel when it was hijacked.

Sri Lanka

Piracy is both an old tradition and a new threat in Sri Lanka. Nonpolitical sea-thieves have reportedly been making off with about $200 million a year in stolen cargo and pil- fered cash boxes year in and year out. While professional pirates operate along the entire coast, they are particularly active off the coast of the country's chief port, Colombo.

The Sea Tigers of the Liberation Tigers of Tamil Eelam (LTTE) is one of the few insurgent navies in the world. It is also one of the most formidable naval forces in the world, ton for ton of craft. An explosion in seagoing attacks by LTTE has made Sri Lankan waters extremely dangerous for every seafarer. The Sea Tiger wing of the rebels, which has always been a force to be reckoned with, began a major offensive in 1996 and 1997. It continues today. Sea Tigers commandeer ships and, in some cases, the crew members. Captured crewmen are routinely held for ransom.

In April 1996 the LTTE staged an abortive attack against the Colombo port and damaged at least three foreign-owned ships. There were no casualties among foreigners, but nine Tigers perished in the suicide attack. In August 1996 the rebels blasted a Philippine-registered cargo ship, the MV *Princess Wave*, with underwater explosives while it was loading mineral sand at Pulmoddai. No one was killed, but the ship was wrecked.

Among the major Sea Tiger targets in 1997 were the 500-seat passenger ferry MV *Misan*, a 3,000-ton merchant ship MV *Morang Bong*, and the MV *Cordiality*. The rebels burned the *Misan*, and the *Morang Bong* was returned to the North Korean government through the Red Cross after weeks of negotiations.

On September 9, 1997, the MV *Cordiality*, a 60,000-ton ore-carrying vessel, was attacked before dawn while anchored a half-mile off the coast at Pulmoddai, north of the Indian Ocean island's eastern port of Trincomalee. The rebels attacked the vessel from three directions while it was loading 29,000 tons of ilmenite. The Tamil Tigers killed 33 crew members and wounded another 17. The *Cordiality*'s accommodation quarters and engine room were reportedly razed by a fire that was set off by rocket-propelled grenades. The ship was left flooded down by the stern.

Navy gunboats patrolling near Trincomalee went to aid the embattled ore-carrier. They fought 15 Tamil rebel gunboats for three hours before driving them off. The government claimed four rebel craft sunk and said three others were damaged.

Other vessels have fallen victim to the rebels' seagoing offensive as well. In late August 1997 a ship loaded with of tens of thousands of mortar shells bound for Sri Lanka was reported missing in the Indian Ocean. The unregistered ship, carrying 32,400 81 mm mortar bombs, disappeared somewhere between Madagascar and Sri Lanka. The exact circumstances were unclear, but investigators speculated that the *Stillus Limmasul*, flying a Greek national flag, could have been intercepted and hijacked by separatist rebels of the LTTE. In addition to the straight-out piracy theory, there was also speculation that the craft could have been one of the "phantom ship" pirates. Far Eastern media reported that the LTTE rebels owned five ships, operating under three international shipping companies in Greece, Cyprus, and Panama. In any event, months later the purloined mortar rounds were dropping around Sri Lankan troopers.

In 1998 the Sea Tigers continued their oceangoing offensive. They used a squadron of suicide boats to blow up Sri Lanka's largest troop transport. While Sri Lankan navy ships are the most likely targets, any vessel in northern Sri Lankan waters is a potential victim of the insurgents. Palk Bay, a strip of sea separating Sri Lanka and India's southern Tamil Nadu state, is a particularly dangerous area for small craft. Sri Lankan navy vessels patrol the area, and high-powered boats belonging to the Sea Tigers also prowl the waters. Contact with either side can be dangerous. Additionally, all vessels in the area stand the chance of unfriendly encounters with the Sri Lankan air patrols that are attempting to halt the piratical Sea Tiger attacks.

The rebels will attack large craft and smaller craft, such as fishing vessels. They make no distinction. Dozens of crewmen, fishermen, and fishing boats have been held hostage.

For example, early in April 1998 the Tamil Tiger guerrillas abducted nine Muslim fishermen in northeastern Sri Lanka and demanded a ransom for their release. Authorities said the sea pirates seized the fishermen off Sampoor in the district of Trincomalee. Three of the fishermen were freed with a message demanding ransom for the freedom of others. The Tigers were asking for 45,000 rupees ($725)—a small fortune in that area—for each of the six Muslim men still held by the LTTE. The fate of those six remains unknown.

Somalia Area

Somalia's coastline has become increasingly dangerous. There have been frequent pirate attacks carried out by people believed to be members of the various warring factions controlling different parts of the country. In this case there is no one there to even attempt to deal with the problem since Somalia has effectively broken up into small "emirates" and has not had a central government since the late dictator Mohamed Siad Barre was overthrown in 1991.

Pirates operating in Somalian waters have not hesitated to blast ships with mortars and grenades. Somalian pirates have sometimes represented—or perhaps misrepresented—themselves as the Somali Coast Guard.

The pirates often board vessels, capture the crew, and then hold the seamen for ransom.

For example, on New Year's Day 1997, armed pirates tried to start out the year with an economic windfall. They attacked a Russian fishing trawler off Somalia but failed to get aboard. The Russians paid an expensive price, however. The captain of the trawler died in the attack.

In November 1997 gunmen stormed a boat moored off the northern Somali coast and kidnapped five aid workers from the United Nations and European Union. The five were eventually released from their unmerited detention only after lengthy negotiations with the waterborne gunmen.

Most vessels such as these—typical of those found in the waters off the Middle East between the Red Sea, Dead Sea, Arabian Sea, and the Indian Ocean—are legitimate. Others are involved in smuggling, and still others are used by pirates to ply their trade.

Late in July 1998 a leader of the Somali Salvation Front freed a pair of French yachtsmen he and his piratical crews had held captive for nearly eight weeks in an isolated village close to the Red Sea in northeast Somalia. The pirate-warlord first demanded a $75,000 ransom for the duo, then upped the ante for "expenses" when the money was not immediately forthcoming. The Frenchmen had been sailing to Madagascar from the French port of Marseilles by way of the Suez Canal and the Red Sea when they were seized at Allula, on the tip of the Horn of Africa.

Other sailors have not been as fortunate as the Frenchmen—receiving "fines" that amount to ransom. They are often tried as "thieves" under the harsh religious law enforced in the area.

Nearby, Kenya and Tanzania have also reported some cases of pirate attacks on ships in their territorial waters. There has been a strong presumption those are spillover attacks from Somalia.

Sierra Leone

Sierra Leone rides a piracy roller coaster. The seaborne violence turns off and on there, making the country a mini-hot spot at times. As in China, the piracy on Sierra Leone waters seems to have a quasi-official tinge; soldiers are known for robbing both boats and cars.

Brazil

Brazil has recently had the distinction of having some of the most pirate-plagued waters in the world. Usually the attackers have been described as heavily armed gangs. Most of the attacks take place when ships are in port or at anchor. But there has been another, even more ominous, pattern: radio calls for help meet with little to no response from authorities.

A typical example of the Brazilian pattern is the March 9, 1997, attack on an Antigua-registered cargo vessel anchored off Rio de Janeiro. The pirates stole part of a cargo of office equipment and made off with cash and other loot valued at $30,000.

In another instance more than a dozen pirates armed with submachine guns used ropes to hoist themselves aboard the container ship *Zim Montevideo* while it was in port at Guanabara Bay on October 21, 1997, then robbed the ship and crew.

Brazil will probably continue to suffer such violence. Authorities have proven indifferent to the problem and the Brazilian coast guard ranks somewhere between invisible and unreliable.

Caribbean Area

Heavily armed men in speedboats have been attacking shrimping boats and other craft off the Nicaraguan coast since the mid-'90s.

Many of the attacks are in Caribbean region near the Nicaragua-Costa Rica border. Those boats are believed to come from Costa Rica and carry an array of impressive military equipment. Other attacks occur throughout the Caribbean.

United States

Piracy in the United States is centered along the Gulf Coast and Florida. Armed gangs, many of them exceptionally violence-prone, attack unwary craft along rivers in Florida and elsewhere in the southeastern quarter.

THE NATURE OF PIRACY

Piracy at sea is really nothing more than a seagoing ambush. As such, piracy is a process. All ambushes, whether at sea or ashore, share common traits. The essentials of an ambush remain the same no matter who the attacker may be, no matter who the intended victim is, no matter where it takes place.

An ambush is a surprise attack upon a moving or temporarily halted target with the mission of destroying or cap-

turing the "enemy" or his possessions. The common element of all ambushes is simple: The quarry is moving, or is stopped somewhere while in the process of moving, when a sudden attack unfolds.

Ambushes are characterized by short, intensely violent action followed by complete and rapid withdrawal. The ambush is not intended to extend over a prolonged period. Normally, the pirate/ambusher will inflict the greatest amount of damage in the initial two or three minutes.

Every book dealing with ambushes repeats "surprise, surprise, surprise" like some mantra. But the "common knowledge" that surprise is the most essential element in an ambush or pirate attack is fatally flawed. *We stress that if there is a single key to a successful ambush, any ambush, it has to be mobility.* Even more than surprise, mobility is the limiting factor for defender and attacker alike.

Defeating modern pirates depends on understanding their tactics and techniques, avoiding surprise, retaining mobility, and depriving the attacker of mobility.

The ambush process involves a seven-step operational sequence:

1) Stalk
2) Site
3) Stop
4) Shock
5) Smother
6) Secure, Search, and Snatch
7) Scram

These seven steps cover, in a general way, all phases of an ambusher's attack—before, during, and after the violence or threat of violence. Every ambush or pirate attack involves these seven steps in some way.

There is no way to affix a time frame to any of the steps. Sometimes a single step in the ambush process may take days or weeks to carry out. In other cases a step may last no more than a fraction of a second. In the case of three of the steps—stop, shock, and smother—the action takes place virtually simultaneously. In many ambushes this trilogy of steps may take less than a minute from initiation to completion. In some cases of an improvised attack, all of the "ambush essentials" may be carried out in less than five minutes.

Stalking and siting are preambush phases of the process. Stalking, in a sense, is the intelligence gathering and planning phase. This is where the ambusher finds out, deduces, or decides where and under what circumstances the victim should be ambushed. After a vessel has been targeted, pirates will move in closer to get more intelligence to build on their assault plan. A complacent crew will not detect this stakeout. A professionally trained crew has a better chance of detecting the surveillance being conducted against their vessel. Siting is the process of moving the attackers or the weapons of attack into the proper place for the attack. Maritime choke points such as straits and island chains are ideal for this tactic. In military parlance this phase is the same as infiltration. Stalking and siting are the two points at which pirate attacks should be stopped.

Stop, shock, and smother take place at the ambush site. This trilogy is at the heart of any attack. To be successful, the ambush target must be halted and prevented from going anywhere—especially from escaping. Ruses or deception are common tactics to make you stop or allow the pirate to come aboard. The ruses can range from a ship claiming to be in distress and asking for assistance to parading a pretty girl in a bikini around another boat or pier in port. Even a pier-side pizza delivery can be used to get aboard. There have been instances where the perpetrator used official uniforms to gain access to the target vessel. This is not unlike the recent slaughter carried out by extremists in Egypt when they killed more than 60 Egyptians and tourists by using police uniforms to move into position prior to opening up on the crowds. Deception has long been a tactic used by the "bad guy" in achieving his objective (see Figure A).

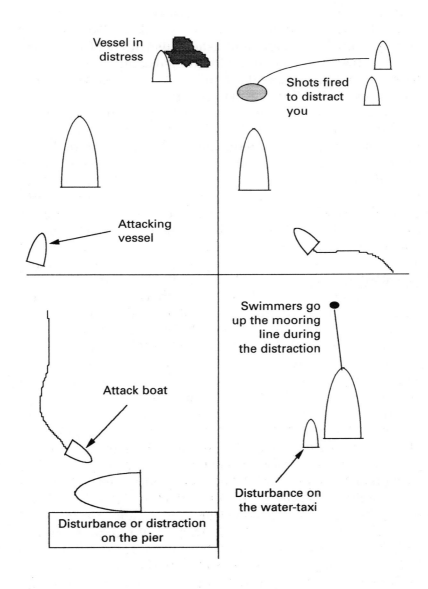

Figure A: Beware of Distractions and Deceptions

Pirates and waterborne terrorists use a variety of diversions, choke points, and screens to get into attack position. They can lay obstacles such as nets or cables. Some will use the low tide in tidal areas to restrict the speed—or even the movement—of craft, attacking in shallow water when deeper drafted vessels cannot move or maneuver. Pirates may also play on Good Samaritan instincts, calling for a vessel to stop to help rescue a "man overboard" or a swimmer in distress. In what is known as a "swarm" tactic, attackers may use many boats at the same time, literally overwhelming their prey by the superior numbers of attackers.

Smother is the part of the ambush or pirate attack that involves overwhelming any initial resistance. This is the last point at which the crew and passengers on a vessel can have any effect on the outcome. While a pirate attack, or any other ambush, may fail after this point, the failure will be due to outside forces.

Secure, search, and snatch are the ambush follow-ups— things such as making certain that none of the quarry have escaped, searching for weapons or papers, and snatching hostages or materials. This phase, too, takes place at the ambush site.

The last phase of an ambush is scram—a descriptive way to define what the military likes to call exfiltration. The more worldly define this step as "getting the hell out of here."

Chapter Two

Maritime Defense:

Beating Them at Their Own Game

The yacht owner or ship operator has a counterplan to follow, a simple operational sequence:

1) Detect
2) Deter
3) Destroy

A pirate can be anybody or any vessel. Vigilance is the key.

Your vessel security personnel need to know every member of the crew, and if guests are expected the security people need to know the details regarding those guests. Such information as their time and means of arrival and nature of their business is vital. Every crew member also has a duty to be aware of—and on the lookout for—suspicious craft or people and then report the information appropriately.

Before going to an area of political unrest and revolt, or one where there are potential risks, do some research to determine the threat level. Where the risk is substantial it is important to ask yourself if you really need to make this trip and thereby put the vessel and crew in harm's way.

Prior to sailing, the owner or operator of any valuable vessel should have a security assessment done on the vessel and crew. This should include an assessment of the proposed sailing plan as well as a study identifying the capabilities of the vessel, equipment, and crew with regard to dealing with maritime bandits. It should point out both strengths and weaknesses and provide recommendations for improving vessel capabilities and training of the crew. The assessment should include recommendations regarding the need for professionals to either train the crew on contingencies or augment the crew, providing enhanced protection during the cruise. Even if the crew is not augmented by professional security personnel, the assessment provides a valuable awareness of the limitations and weaknesses of the vessel and crew.

Prior to getting under way, the captain of any vessel sailing in pirate-potential waters should get all hands on board together for a presail meeting. The agenda should include the following:

- Purpose of sailing
- The vessel's itinerary, including length of time
- Ports of call
- Standard operating procedures for crew and guests aboard
- Attack philosophy—the techniques and tactics common to pirates in these waters
- The role to be played by each individual
- Intelligence briefing of the area (geopolitical, cultural, etc.)
- Threat briefing regarding the pirates of this region
- Navigational briefing (including tracks, time lines, and filing a sailing plan)
- Common brief of who to contact, schedule for radio checks, communications planning
- Any changes to the plan once underway
- Port visitation policies and security measures

No matter where you are, in safe harbor or dangerous waters, being observant and sharpening the crew's powers of observation are essential. Only after the threat has been detected can the pirates be deterred. Detection requires a mix of good watch procedures, competent personnel, and adequate equipment. Such things as a good radar watch, brilliant all-around lighting of the water near the yacht while at anchor, night vision devices (NVDs) for improving the visual acuity of watchstanders, intrusion detection devices (IDDs) to detect intruders, and compressed air horns for instantaneous alerting of everyone aboard the craft—passengers and crew—in case of trouble, are a must.

A watch, quarter, and station bill should be made out to repel boarders under way and in port. The crew must prepare by employing some of the following measures:

- Making certain that boarding ladders are locked in their up position at night
- Ensuring that anchor cables don't allow attackers easy access to the deck
- Making it difficult for a craft of any size, or even swimmers, to approach the anchored vessel without being spotted
- Securing access hatches and portals to the interior

Watchstanders have to move around the ship, checking over the side often, particularly in those areas where boarders would be most likely to put their boat or raft while they sneak aboard. Favorite weak spots include the stern and anywhere the ship's bulk overhangs the water. The ship's boarding ladder should be well-secured—and locked into place if possible—so that pirates cannot simply snip the cable and have the stairway rumble down to greet them.

In the case of open ocean steaming, radar is one of the best detection devices. A good lookout is second. If a craft's path converges with your vessel and you are suspicious, increase your speed and attempt to exit the area. Assume anything coming close to you, particularly at high speed, is a threat. Reverse course if necessary to avoid contact with incoming vessels. If vessels maneuver in an attempt to block your vessel, zigzag through at flank speed. Ramming the other vessel may become necessary.

The first key to thwarting pirates is to detect any possible attack before seagoing ruffians can get alongside the hull, and certainly before they can get aboard.

The boat's deck is a dividing line of sorts. When pirates are still trying to get on deck, you, as the defender, have the advantage. When the attackers gain deck the odds will shift. Even though the advantage is not always in favor of the attacker at that point, it is still true that those on the vessel have lost much of their previous advantage.

One of the greatest deterrents to pirates is loss of the element of surprise. If they know they have been spotted—particularly if they are aware that they have been seen and that countermeasures are being taken even before they have made an effective and aggressive move—they are likely to back off and wait for some less-observant crew to come their way. Demonstrating that the crew and vessel are prepared and alert is a key element of deterrence.

In harbor or at anchor one of the greatest assets to deterring piracy is the proper use of the launch that moves crew and guests ashore and back. Once any approaching craft enters a perimeter security zone, the launch can and should be used to intercept it.

When used as a floating interceptor, the launch deters the curious and the dangerous from approaching the vessel. Moreover the use of a stand-off launch sends a message that the crew is alert and not a willing target of opportunity, prompting most would-be attackers to go elsewhere in search of victims. The launch is not a means of stopping pirates; it is an early-warning device. An approaching craft that evades the launch must be considered dangerous.

Generally the launch should have a native speaker aboard if possible. The craft leaves the mother ship and approaches an incoming vessel, requesting that it lay off and depart the area of the larger vessel for security reasons. Communications back to the vessel from the launch can be used to report anything suspicious noted during the approach to the intruding vessel.

The launch can also be used when alongside a pier to check under/around the pier and in conducting antiswimmer operations. The launch can approach an unfamiliar pier, check for security, and guide the vessel to the best pier-side approach. It can also assist in line handling for the vessel.

Effective launch operations require the following:

- Good communications between the vessel and launch and any other links in the system
- A powerful spotlight or flashlight that is fully charged or supplied with fresh batteries
- A loudspeaker system
- Flashing lights or similar strobe or lighting systems
- A native speaker or someone familiar with the appropriate phrases
- Shotgun or other appropriate weapon systems where legally permitted
- A qualified crew of two individuals, at a minimum

At anchor or in port, the engineering department and deck crew can help deter attacks by swimmers. Randomly turning the sea suction intakes on and off or turning the screws keeps most swimmers at a distance. Fire hoses can be employed against boarders as well. Occasionally dropping M-80 firecrackers with weights over the sides and dangling grappling hooks or even the larger fishing hooks can also deter approaching swimmers.

If attackers should succeed in coming alongside an anchored vessel, the watch can twist the vessel in place by running engines at the highest RPM possible. This makes it extremely difficult for attackers to come aboard, especially if they employ many boats. At anchor or alongside a pier, the watch should use flares, sirens, and other lighting, such as strobe lights or search lights, to attract attention to the attempts of the attackers. Those too are deterrents.

Destroy is the last resort for the mariner, but that is not the end game move. Pleasure boaters or merchant seamen should not have to do the work of coast guards or the military. The ideal is always to detect any attack in good time, escape from the pirates, and exit the area. Notify local or international authorities and provide all observations to them—that is the best outcome. But if attackers are detected and even then refuse to be deterred, they may be destroyed in self-defense.

PREPARING FOR TROUBLE

The captain and crew of any high-value vessel—particularly one carrying people who have ransom potential—have to be prepared and properly trained.

The captain and crew must train as a team; they must work as a team. In something as complex as counter-boarding operations, leaving operations to instincts, snap judgments, or even dumb luck is unwise. The crew must have a defense plan and be versed in that plan. But a crew also needs the tools to fight back, the tools to deter an armed attacker.

Usually the captain and crew of a yacht should be armed with weapons that would allow them to resist anything smaller than a naval gunboat. The vessel's crew must have experience, and they must have conducted drills for all contingencies. Planning, and then exercising the knowledge, pays instant bonuses if the vessel faces pirates of any kind.

Detection Equipment

No specific piece of equipment can be a panacea in detecting approaching trouble. Therefore, all available resources have to be used simultaneously, creating an effective detection system.

Radars that are well tuned to detect small and large craft alike are among the most effective tools. These can warn of the approach of dangerous craft in time to launch an effective defense against the intruders. Radars should be used for this purpose while under way at sea, when anchored, or when moored in port.

The approach angle of vessels will often indicate a threat or potential problem, and the crew should be trained in the use of the radar to detect potential problems. Crews also need to understand the limitations of radar. One weak spot of most radars is a "blind" spot just behind the antenna. The blind spot results from mounting the antenna on the forward part of the mast, where it is most effective for navigating the ship. Because this blind spot is well-known and often used by attackers, an alert 360-degree watch—that can make frequent checks aft of the vessel, in the radar's blind spot, to ensure that nothing is approaching from that direction—is vital.

Vision aids such as binoculars, night vision devices, thermal image systems, and, most importantly, the MK 1 Mod 0 human eyeball are very effective in detecting approaching piracy problems before they get too close. Alertness of the individual is the key here. The alertness should be at a heightened state in areas known for piracy.

Sonar offers less of a chance of detecting pirates under normal circumstances but can still be effective in certain

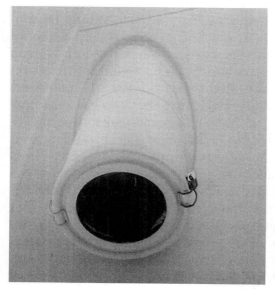

A marinized closed-circuit TV can be used to observe hard-to-watch areas on the vessel or monitor boarding ladders and gangway accesses to the vessel.

instances. Sonar may detect the noise of an approaching vessel engine, and in rare instances it has proven effective in detecting approaching small submersibles or divers. (Divers or submersibles may be used to destroy or damage the vessel and crew, or to plant drugs at one port only to be removed at the next port. The sophistication of drug runners, pirates, or other seagoing criminals cannot be underestimated.)

Intrusion detection devices (overside, on deck, and inside) can include infrared sensors, pressure pads, closed circuit television cameras, microphones, magnetic strips, and trip wires. All of these can be effective in detecting perpetrators, both in port and while under way. These should be used in conjunction with proper external and internal lighting. In most instances intrusion detection devices are fairly inexpensive and highly effective, dollar for dollar.

Intrusion devices can help protect any vessel, but they are particularly needed on vessels manned by small crews or ships that have large areas that cannot easily be viewed from the bridge or quarterdeck.

Weapons—Lethal and Nonlethal

Lethal weapons are among the tools that should be considered when planning to ward off pirates. Weapons should be placed aboard—and kept locked—while the ship is in an American port. Weapons and sufficient ammunition supplies should always be brought aboard *before* the craft sails for foreign ports. Many boat owners have found how extremely difficult it can be to bring weapons aboard a U.S. vessel legally while docked in a foreign port. Most countries have restrictions on the possession of weapons, or at least possession by noncitizens, and trying to bring weapons aboard the vessel at locations outside the United States can range from difficult to impossible.

There is no single weapon that will work best in all cases. A combination of weapons is needed for the weapons suite on yachts and other ships. The well-stocked ship's arsenal should include handguns, rifles, and shotguns.

During a stopover in Malaysia, Vantage Systems, Inc. (VSI) instructor Jim Kauber trains the captain of a mega-yacht (Capt. Frank Gillies of the MY Michaela Rose) *in defense against pirate attacks with a shotgun.*

However, the first point to understand is that weapons are only as good as the shooter.

Using weapons in real life is not something from a Hollywood movie. Hitting a target with any weapon is difficult at any time, but accuracy is particularly difficult when the shooter is on a rocking, rolling deck on the high seas.

The handgun is easily carried by a watch, particularly in ports where that is permitted. Handguns are easy to access, and unlike larger weapons, they are easy to carry around the vessel. However, unless the shooter is a trained marksman, the handgun is often ineffective as a defensive weapon to keep intruders off the ship.

Handguns usually come into their own when used for self-defense after attackers have already penetrated the vessel. By contrast, the rifle—particularly a semiautomatic 7.62 mm rifle—is effective in repelling boarders or intruders before they gain the deck. The rifle has fair range and good penetration. In the hands of a trained marksman the rifle can be quite effective.

But the single best all-around weapon for defense of the yacht is a stainless steel 12-gauge shotgun—the stainless part being to minimize the effects of the environment on the weapon.

Handguns are too inaccurate for even close-quarter battle at sea, except in the hands of expert marksmen. Rifles may be useful in trying to keep the attackers at some distance from the vessel, but again, they tend to be inaccurate when fired from a heaving, rolling ship. Shotguns, however, provide good target acquisition up to at least 25 meters. The shot pattern gives a wide area of coverage. When rifled slugs are available, the shotgun can be used effectively against the wheelhouse, engine spaces, and even the hull of many attacking craft.

The yacht should carry a supply of various types of shotgun ammunition—including rifled slugs—but the standard load for the weapons is generally #4 or 00 buck. Plan for enough ammunition to permit frequent and substantial training and practice.

Each vessel owner and captain has to establish a standard operating policy for the use and storage of weapons:

• What weapons will be aboard?
• Who will be trained to use them?
• Who will be authorized to use them?
• Where is each weapon post on board?
• Under what circumstances will they be used?
• Will they be kept locked in their location(s)?
• Where will they be placed for easy access?
• How will the countries visited regulate their existence?
• When will they be kept at the ready?

Nonlethal stand-off weapons for use against boarders include high-pressure fire hoses, flare guns, and blinding lights directed at the eyes of attackers. When obtainable, flash-bang grenades and riot tear gas guns can be effectively used to deter and confuse boarders. Electronic stun guns and pepper gas sprays may be effective at close range, but if pirates are close enough for these to be useful, resistance has become a hand-to-hand affair and is probably a lost cause. (Don't forget to take the wind direction into account when using tear gas or sprays.)

Molotov cocktails—any of the improved kind that do not require an open flame but use flares or chemicals for ignition—may also be used at close quarters. Smoke floats are another possibility to confuse the perpetrators with regard to the location and approach of their vessel against yours.

Among the nonlethal weapons, we recommend such items as OC-10 pepper gas, batons, and electronic stun guns of at least 120,000 volts of power.

The defense against pirates should take their strong and weak points, as well as your strong and weak points, into account. Remember, a boat, yacht, or ship is only as well protected as its crew is effective.

Detection

Detection is a two-edged sword. If pirates can't detect you, they cannot board you. If you can't detect them, they can get close enough to board you.

The yacht owner traveling in piracy-prone areas may want to consider ways of reducing detectability. Moreover, the yacht owner will certainly want to understand the limits of his or her own detection systems.

A mega-yacht usually has the cruising range of a ship. In troubled waters the best technique is to stay well out to sea, avoiding the coastline and staying out of striking range of small craft. Planned sailing tracks, based upon good intelligence, can greatly assist in avoiding confrontations at sea.

Expect pirates to have some sophistication. They have improved their own techniques through the years since the black flag flew over the Spanish Main. Expect that they will have aboard (as you should) at least the following:

- Field glasses
- Night vision devices
- Radar

Vision

Visual spotting is dependent upon sea state, the blending of your boat into the sea, sky condition, clarity of the horizon, and the time of day. The color of your hull and masts, if they do not blend in with the background, may well be a detriment. Many parts on a boat will reflect light like a mirror, pinpointing your location to people who might otherwise miss your craft completely. Anyone can get crazy about things like this. Windscreens, for instance, have high reflectability. So does chrome. So who is going to take out the windows or paint the fittings flat black? How serious a detriment these are to safety is really an open question—and even cherry red masts would not be a problem unless and until you run into a pirate. Choosing a color scheme and reducing reflectivity to reduce detectability is not a bad idea for yacht owners—many of the pirates do it—but whether this would really prove worthwhile is more a matter of the owner's point of view than any other consideration.

Visual detectability actually depends upon more than just detection of the vessel itself. The wake is highly detectable. This is becoming even more of a factor because of today's modern technology. Thermal imaging devices are available that can detect even minute differences in temperature, such as found in wakes where the water aft a moving boat is in fact quite different in temperature from the surrounding sea.

Even without thermal detection devices, the wake and spray generated by small craft provide the principal visual indicators. As a rule of thumb, Sea State Three and speeds of less than two knots will normally eliminate wake as a means of detection. The waves create enough surface disruption to mask it.

Here again, disguising the wake is a more important factor for the successful pirate than it is to the potential victim. No yacht owner is going to dog-paddle his craft around the seven seas in Sea State Three and above just to eliminate the possibility of wake detection.

The high visibility of a wake works against the pirate attempting to attack an anchored yacht. Because of wake visibility, in certain circumstances any would-be pirate may have to approach at slow speed, or the pirate craft may even have to float down on the tide to get alongside the victim's boat. Instead of motors, pirates may use paddles or poles to propel an ambush craft. Tidal flow and current can also be used to quietly drift the boats, and the attackers aboard the boats, into the proper position. But all those things take time—and the extra time gives the defenders more time to spot the intruder. That is why alert, all-around watches while at anchor are so important.

Bioluminescence, or the production of light by minute marine life such as certain types of plankton, is another means of visual detection. The bioluminescent scar is generally most visible on dark nights with high cloud cover and low sea state. Higher sea states and a bright moon or stars reflecting off the ocean surface virtually eliminate any chance bioluminescence can be used for detecting the approach of a pirate vessel.

The ability of starlight scopes or night vision goggles (NVGs) to detect a small craft—or any object—depends on the amount of ambient light available. But under a half moon, by rule of thumb, small craft may be detectable at one-half mile or more.

From a defensive standpoint it is important to remember that terrain masking and camouflage may be used to hide pirates. They can lurk in a cove, hidden against the backdrop of the land, until a potential victim passes close beside. Then they may come pelting out. Watching the water's edge of nearby land formations for any movement is important when transiting pirate-prone waters.

YACHT EQUIPMENT

Yacht equipment should include a lighting system that will allow for constant illumination of the water around an anchored craft. In addition, yachts should have spotlights that can cover 360 degrees.

Boarding gangways should always be in their "up" position during the night or during any period of reduced visibility. Where technically possible, boarding ladders should be locked into place or braced so that simply snipping a cable will not release them.

Anchor cables or other lines extending from the ship should not facilitate surreptitious boarding of the ship. Cones and razor wire can effectively close those up as entry points.

Radar should be in good working order, optimally tuned for the conditions, and constantly monitored even at anchor to spot approaching small vessels.

Most ships rely heavily on radar to detect potential pirates. Captains and crew monitor the radar for unidentified blips—especially ones that are moving fast or are on an intercept course. (Anything moving on an intercept course should be treated as if it were carrying a boarding party.) But the fact is that radar is only marginally capable of detecting the type of small craft many pirates use. The captain of a ship has to wring the most out of his set. Tuning and reading the radar, then, become all important.

Every radar has its blind spots, and those vary—not only with the radar but with the weather conditions and sea state. It is important to test the yacht radar against a target craft to see where the weak spots occur in your radar coverage and to plug those holes. When detection capability tests have not been carried out, assume that the radar cannot pick up a blip from a small craft within 500 yards of the yacht, or beyond 7,000 yards. An area of reduced/denied detection is often directly to the stern of the ship in the 170- to 180-degree relative region. For that reason stern watches are critical, whether the vessel is anchored or in transit.

When possible, pirates may choose periods of higher sea state (three and above) to minimize the probability of detection. Not only is it more difficult to visually spot the approach of a small craft, the already degraded radar operation is further exploited by reducing the approach speed to mask signatures in the sea clutter. The general rule is the less wake the better when approaching a target vessel.

While bow-on penetration is generally preferred, since it usually minimizes radar cross section, the fact is that when small craft operate in a zigzag pattern they are often more difficult to detect and track. This is due to the inability of radar operators to establish a constant track from which to project target location.

Small craft traveling parallel to the direction of the swell are generally more detectable by radar than those running perpendicular to it. Marauders know it—through the fraternity of thugs and from individual experience—and are likely to make use of that fact.

Small pirate vessels can avoid radar detection by operating at or near channel markers or other large buoys. The radar's return off the pirate will often be confused with, or masked by, the one off the buoy. Radar does not do a good job of discriminating between a buoy and a small craft in close proximity, nor will it determine that small craft are located at a buoy. This is another reason an alert lookout watch must be stood.

Vision-enhancing equipment such as good binoculars and NVDs should be available to all watchstanders in pirate-prone areas.

New polymer interior coating on the glass on the bridge inside portholes provides a degree of protection from small arms fire, shrapnel, and flying glass. It is an after-market add-on and reasonably priced.

Compressed-air horns are needed for warning the rest of the boat about problems. Effective means of resistance should be available to the crew—just in case events come down to that. Small handheld radios should be an integral part of yachting or shipping. These have an important role in all inter-vessel communications, but they become particularly important in antipiracy actions.

DEFENSE STRATEGY AGAINST THE
TWO BASIC ATTACK PROFILES

There are really only two basic strategies of aggression: urgent and deliberate attacks.

An urgent attack would be most often associated with a military patrol boat or a heavily armed pirate craft that believes it is far better armed and faster than its prey. Terrorists conducting a suicide attack would also be likely to adopt this method of attack. In the urgent type of attack the vessel closes on the yacht at high speed, over a long straight course. The pirate makes little use of cover, concealment, or deception. The high-speed inbound contact—usually from radar, vision, or sometimes sound—gives target ships a good indication that the contact has potentially hostile intent.

Any high-speed inbound radar target, or one converging on your course, is highly suspect. Watching the vessel can give further indications of hostility. Key indicators include the following:

- A weapons mount (or covered area that could house a heavy weapon) in the bow
- Visible arms in the craft
- Disguises or masking of the crew's faces
- An exceptionally large crew for the size of the craft
- Motors larger than would normally be found on that type of craft

When you are faced with an urgent attack style, the best move is to run, call for assistance, and immediately prepare to repel boarders.

The deliberate attack is often much more complex and convoluted. The deliberate attack is subject to an almost unlimited number of variations and permutations and may involve a number of pirate or terrorist craft.

Prepositioning of the attack craft may be used, in which case the attacker may not move at all. Instead the attackers carefully place their craft, or use ruses, so that the target ship will drive down on the attack craft's position. That eliminates the need for the attacker to make a long or obvious approach. Slow relative speeds used in prepositioning allow the attacking vessel to slowly close on the target ship in a nonthreatening manner.

High-speed stern chases or bow approaches with lights blacked out in heavy weather, which masks detection, may also be used in the deliberate attack.

Other cover and deception measures most commonly used in a deliberate attack include the following:

- Turning off all navigation lights and darkening the ship
- Using zigzag approach courses
- Employing deceptive lighting such as fishing lights or dive lights
- Rafting up with local fishing craft or lying in ambush in a cove
- Using merchant traffic for screening
- Making judicious use of speed—either fast or slow
- Ruses to encourage you to stop your vessel

In any case, no matter which type of attack is used, whether the attack takes place in the open ocean or in a harbor, the target vessel usually must be boarded or surrendered. *Pirates cannot achieve success unless they come aboard the target vessel.* For that reason it makes sense to think of the hull and gunwales of a yacht as castle walls. As long as they are not breached, as long as the raiders do not reach the deck of the yacht, the defenders are in the most powerful position.

Establishing an effective antipiracy plan requires the captain to draw up a watch quarter station bill that takes piracy and pirates into account. Everybody is a lookout—no matter where he or she is.

For a yacht the antipiracy plan involves drawing concentric circles around the ship. The first circle extends up to three miles out from your yacht. You want to be aware of anything or anyone within that circle; you need to observe all other vessels for suspicious activity. The radar watch, as well as visual identification, is important here. However it is as important to avoid paranoia as it is to avoid complacency. There is no room on a ship for either. Since there are relatively few pirates in comparison with the number of boats throughout the world, there is generally little cause for alarm with regard to nearby craft. If they're more than a mile away they have little ability to hurt you. Pirates have to get in closer—preferably without being seen. Terrorists have to move in closer as well. For those reasons, the first, and the best, clue to potential trouble is any boat moving closer to you.

At about a mile out, any ship (not just those traveling at high speed) that appears to be on an approaching or collision course should be considered a potential boarder. At that point all available crew and even passengers should appear on deck—watching in the direction from which the perceived threat is coming. The more eyes the better. Pirates often rely on stealth and on the failure of the victim to see them until it is too late for effective action. The simple act of mustering passengers and crew along a rail, looking at the suspicious boat, will cause many pirates to give up the attack and seek some other less alert, less troublesome, target. Most piracy is nothing more than a seagoing ambush. If pirates can't take your vessel—and those aboard—by surprise, they are already in serious trouble. They know it. When you clearly demonstrate to them that they have been seen and are being watched carefully, they will usually go elsewhere in search of less observant seafarers and other shipping targets.

There is one caveat to putting all hands on deck looking at an approaching ship: make certain that the obvious approach is not being used to distract everyone so that a surprise attack can be mounted from another direction. In other words, maintain 360-degree security at all times. Keep an eye on the known intruder into your sea space, but at the same time be aware of any other vessels that may approach—or that you may be approaching unwittingly.

When the approaching vessel reaches the mile-out point, the nonlethal weaponry such as fire hoses should be broken out and placed at strategic locations while designated crew members stand by to use them.

At a quarter-mile, five minutes from potential contact (or when it is apparent that the approaching vessel is on a collision course), assigned crew should go into action stations.

- The approaching vessel should be warned off by lights, signal flags, voice communication, or radio.
- At least one person should be designated to send an emergency radio transmission, making certain to give the location, the name of your vessel, and particulars about the suspicious vessel. While the message may not actually be transmitted yet if your preparations and communications are monitored (and they will be if the approaching craft is a pirate vessel), the intimations that a distress call is being prepared tend to end the matter right there.
- Those people aboard the ship who have been designated as noncombatants should leave the deck and go to their quarters.
- Weapons should be brought to the deck and distributed to those people—crew and any passengers—assigned to repel the boarding party. The defenders should seek cover where possible and concealment where cover is not available.
- Aggressive maneuvering of the vessel should start, making it difficult for unfriendly craft to come alongside. Fishtailing while traveling at the highest safe speed is often useful.

Maneuvering at all in close quarters requires some deftness. Most captains are taught to avoid collisions with another vessel at all costs. Yet when trying to fend off a

During these maneuvers, all other anti-boarding measures are also being used to include radio, flares, distress horns, and finally, weapons release authorization

Attacking craft

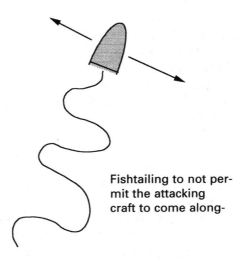

Fishtailing to not permit the attacking craft to come along-

Figure B: Aggressive Maneuvers

boarding party the smartest thing may well be to collide with the attacking craft, particularly if it is smaller and may not stand up well in an encounter.

The attackers are expecting you to try to escape, and their plans have probably been based on the assumption that you will attempt to get away from them, not come closer to them. Depending on the height of your hull above the waterline, as well as the relative height of their deck, turning into them when you are on a parallel course, or across their intended course at close range, may disrupt the aim of any gunmen or knock potential boarders off their feet. Such a maneuver is almost guaranteed to cause a radical change of direction on their part unless they have no fears about the outcome of any collision.

Ramming is a subject few people want to talk about—rules of the road are part of the 10 commandments of seamanship and have been for millennia. But ramming an attacker is a viable defense.

The key to ramming a craft is to strike a glancing blow. Do not attempt to run over the pirate vessel or cut the craft in half; the debris from the collision may damage your screws and struts, thereby decreasing your speed or halting your escape entirely.

Other defensive tactics include the following:

- Executing a fishtail maneuver, i.e., going both fast and slow and other irregular course changes. (This makes boarding a severe hazard and may discourage the best pirate boat captain from coming alongside.)
- Blinding the pirate vessel's coxswain with a spotlight or with flares shot directly at him in nighttime attacks.
- Simultaneously employing all techniques and lethal/nonlethal weapons to stop the pirates from coming onboard.

Any signs of an attempted forcible boarding, such as the employment of grappling hooks or any gunfire from the intruder, should be considered active aggression. In that circumstance defenders may fire at will and as their targets allow. A gunfight at sea is not the goal of antipiracy procedures, however, and should be considered the very last, improbable outcome. Nor is your purpose to capture any seagoing desperadoes and bring them in for justice. That's a job for coast guards.

In the event of an attempted forcible boarding, the goal for your craft and crew is simple: get out of there in one piece. Speeding away, maneuvering, and discouraging their boarding are the hallmarks of the battle after that point.

On the closer approach of any suspicious vessel—at approximately one minute from probable contact—a flare should be fired across the bow of the offending craft, followed by a rifle shot or shotgun blast. The distress call should now be made (it can always be retracted if necessary) if the intruder does not shear off or attempts to approach from a new angle. Contact by radio, a distress call, firing red flares in the air, illumination, and sounding distress horns should continue. Pirates do not want outside attention attracted to their illegal actions.

THE BOTTOM LINE

By now the captain has to make a decision whether to surrender, fight, or take flight. In almost all cases the best thing—if the option is still open—is to flee while calling for assistance. Any decision to resist is much more complicated.

The decision to resist is based on the expected chances of success and an appraisal of whether the attackers are likely to physically harm the crew and passengers even if no resistance is offered.

If a member of the piratical boarding party is killed, injured, or maimed in the process, and the pirates do succeed in taking over the boat, passengers or crew may be killed or injured in angry retaliation. In addition, there is a chance of incurring casualties among the boat's passengers or crew during the battle. But once gunfire has been exchanged, and particularly if the spirited defense has caused casualties among the pirates, there should be no consideration of ending the resistance.

It is probably too late to make the decision to resist once people are swarming over the taffrail. If they are already aboard by the time anyone notices them, the pirates have probably effectively taken over the ship. Few captains can organize an effective resistance in the few moments available between boarding and the seizure of the wheelhouse and/or engineering spaces.

Running away—usually the best move—is as fraught with problems as fighting.

Keep in mind that those people aboard the intruder vessel probably know the geography of the area intimately—or at least far better than you do if you are just transiting. For that reason high-speed maneuvering in shoaling water is not recommended. On the open ocean there may be some advantage to ringing up flank speed and trying to escape simply by speed, particularly if the attack craft do not appear to be capable of keeping up with yours. But in coastal waters the combination of high speed and a lack of attention to proper navigation can result in the loss of the ship. In fact, the pirates may be hoping that you will go aground in your haste to flee. Running aground would put you at their mercy since their vessels are usually more shallow-drafted. Then they could maneuver around and board your wreck.

Chapter Three

Narrow Waterway Ship Attacks

Narrow waterway ship attacks are used by terrorists rather than pirates. While these attacks are ambushes too, they are usually designed to do damage and kill. Attackers use stand-off weapons against people and the craft; destruction and death, not robbery, is the aim.

A HISTORY OF VIOLENCE

The technique of ambushing watercraft as they move along inland waterways has been used by Muslim fundamentalists in Egypt to help destroy the tourist industry. While many of those attacks failed in every tactical sense, they resulted in a publicity coup. They were highly successful in the strategic sense. For that reason they are likely to be repeated by terrorists and rebels elsewhere.

Starting in mid-1992 Muslim militants in Egypt mounted a highly effective ambush campaign that targeted tourists and the tourist trade. These were the major producers of foreign exchange for the nation and the economic mainspring of the country. The militant campaign was as simple as it was effective. The weapons—guns and bombs—were simple, effective, and easy to obtain. This inventive ambush campaign, carried out by a handful of people, vetted the country's tourist industry within a matter of months. Boats and river craft were among the targets.

On October 2, 1992, the organization known as Gama'a attacked a Nile cruiser ferrying 140 Germans on a placid cruise along the river. Three Egyptian crew members were wounded in that waterway ambush.

On April 9 of the following year, ambushers were back blasting at boats in a revival of riverine ambush. The Gama'a militants fired at a Nile cruiser carrying 41 Germans near Assiut. Nobody was injured.

On September 18 gunmen opened fire on a Nile cruiser as it navigated through the troubled southern province of Assiut, Egypt's chief stronghold of Muslim militants. Militants opened fire on the boat, which was carrying 22 French tourists, blasting away from positions along the banks. They missed, security sources said. Other reports said the ambushers, who fired from the banks of a plantation, broke one of the craft's windows. The two things everyone seemed to agree on was that no casualties were reported among tourists aboard the ship and that the attackers got a lot of publicity—worldwide notoriety, in fact. An attack against a yacht would be just as effective.

Rivers, canals and sloughs, and other restricted waterways all make effective killing zones. The riverine environment quite often lends itself to attacks. The ambush along a river or waterway requires fewer logistics than almost any other common type. Waterway ambushes can be staged with very few to no rockets, small amounts of ammunition, and little or no explosives.

The climate along many waterways is temperate, a factor that favors ambushing forces because they can remain immobile, in place, for lengthy periods of time without experiencing severe discomfort. At the same time the terrain usually favors using the ambush as a tactic. Generally a river has a plethora of locations where cover and concealment can be found. An attacker almost always has clear field of fire. Because rivers are natural channels that widen and narrow, often significantly, rivers have natural "choke points" that can be easily exploited.

A good waterway ambush is easiest when the cover afforded by the river environment is used well. High banks, trees, bends in the river, islands, and rocks all make excellent cover. Islands and obstructing rocks in the waterway may channelize boats into waters where maneuverability is restricted. Narrow waterway ambushes most often occur near bends in the river. At bends the control of the craft is more difficult and the river channel generally runs closer to one shore than the other, forcing the craft out of the middle of the waterway and toward the shore.

While riverine ambushes—including attacks on watercraft plying rivers, sloughs, and streams—can be extremely simple, they are often much more complex. Riverine ambushes are often multiple-pointed. A series of ambushes may be mounted from the shore using rockets, command- or contact-detonated explosives, and automatic weapons. Typically, the boat will attempt to speed from the killing zone, only to move into another ambush.

DEFENSIVE MEASURES

Just as the typical pirate attack differs from the typical terrorist or rebel attack, the response of captain, crew, and passengers is also different in a narrow waterway attack.

This vessel is typical of the high-speed, more modern type of pirate craft used to prey on vessels near shore or in restricted waterways.

The key points in defending against an ambush in restricted waters are as follows:

- Get people under cover
- Call for assistance
- Maneuver out of the area at safe speeds
- Fire red distress flares, initiate Grimes lights and strobes, set off the ship's horn so that other craft in the area know you are in distress
- Illuminate their craft and yours to attract attention to your dilemma
- Return fire if weapons are used against you and if they are available

Of course, the best move is to avoid narrow waterway attacks by avoiding all areas where they may occur. If you must go into a danger area, plan your course track carefully along the narrow waterways. Use most-used routes with a large amount of traffic. Plan to sail when traffic is heaviest. Being alone and sailing in uninhabited waterways attracts specific attention to your vessel.

Chapter Four

Supplemental Assistance

In pirate-prone waters, the extra eyes of supplemental help, trained to look for suspicious activity, are a desirable addition to the ship.

Other crew members have as their primary job the running of the ship and the providing of comfort to the guests aboard the yacht. For them security is, at best, an additional duty that has a low priority. Supplemental staff, however, have no higher priority than assuring the safety of the ship and those aboard.

When integrated with a vessel's complement of guests and crew, professionals are not a burden to the crew, but rather provide enhancement to the daily operations by performing such duties as watchstanding under way and in port, operating the vessel's small craft, assisting the owners and guests in SCUBA diving, handling of lines, underwater hull inspection and repair, and numerous other maritime disciplines.

Supplemental security personnel provide professional training and teach awareness to the crew so that they are prepared to act positively and instinctively in security situations even when they are not augmented by security personnel. Owners and guests feel more comfortable and relaxed when they do not have to be concerned for vessel security in their voyages. Increased security opens new, exciting cruising areas where owners and guests can experience the local adventure and ambiance without the fear of piracy, extortion, and pilferage. Mariners don't leave port without lifeboats and survival equipment—though they hope and expect they will never need them. In some parts of the world the risks of sailing need to be met with a "security lifeboat" provided by a security contingent.

Chapter Five

Checklists

ALERT STAGES

The following stages permit the vessel to set itself at certain conditions of readiness depending upon the potential threat that it may be going under or the risk level of the area it may be transiting.

Yellow Alert: Three-mile detection; focused radar and lookouts on contact, and 360-degree watch.

Orange Alert: Repel boarder stations. You have five minutes or less to man up these stations and have equipment ready.

Red Alert: All antipiracy measures are being put into effect at the captain's call to keep craft from coming alongside.

Note: The Watch Quarter and Station Bill identifies every member of the crew, his particular assignment, and what he provides in each of the three stages of alert.

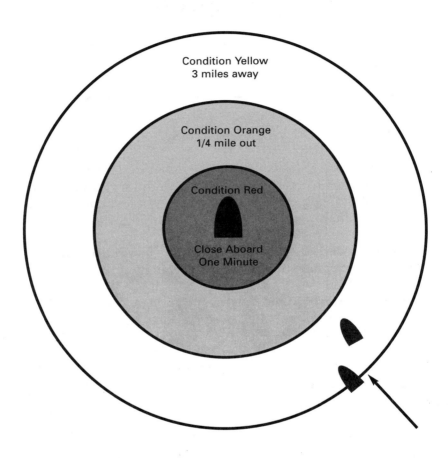

Condition Yellow
3 miles away

Condition Orange
1/4 mile out

Condition Red

Close Aboard
One Minute

MAINTAIN A 360° WATCH
There may be more than
one threat situation

Figure C: Conditional Alert Stages for Incoming Threats

PRESAILING PREPARATION

Detection Equipment
- Binocular
- Radar
- Night vision devices
- Intrusion detection systems

Antiboarding Measures
- Firearms
- Physical systems

Nonlethal Weapons
- Batons
- Pepper gas
- Stun guns
- Fire hoses, charged

Route Planning
- Presailing planning—intelligence of the area through various sources
- U.S. Embassy should let you know if the local officials are corrupt
- Lay out your track and file from port of departure to port of destination
- Link up with other vessels during transit through dangerous waters

MARINER'S CHEAT SHEET OF
ANTIPIRACY PROCEDURES

☑ Call for assistance at the first signs of trouble.

☑ Have antiboarding systems such as high-pressure hoses ready.

☑ Maneuver out of the danger area at the highest safe speed.

☑ "Fishtail" the boat to make boarding more difficult.

☑ Fire Red Distress Flares, initiate Grimes lights and strobes, and set off the ship's horn so that other craft in the area know you are in distress.

☑ Illuminate your craft to attract attention to it.

☑ Return fire if weapons are used against you and if you have weapons available.

☑ Use the most frequently used routes with a large amount of traffic and sail through those areas when traffic is heaviest. Being alone and in uninhabited waterways attracts specific attention to your vessel.

About the Authors

Mr. Jim Gray is a combat veteran in small combatant craft from the deltas in Vietnam to the unusual type of sea battles encountered in the Persian Gulf. He has spent nearly 22 years in the U.S. Navy as an active-duty and reserve specialist serving in the elite navy special operations combatant craft community. His tactical, hands-on expertise is unsurpassed. Mr. Gray was instrumental in developing a more effective plan for deploying and patrolling with the navy MK III gunboats in the Persian Gulf during the Iran-Iraq wars of 1987-89. For that effort, recognition was received for his command from the theater commander in charge of all U.S. forces serving in the Persian Gulf. He continues to train special boat crewmen in tactical operation of combatant craft.

Mr. Mark Monday has spent more than 27 years studying and analyzing terrorists and insurgents throughout the world. During the past five years his concentration has focused on maritime terrorism. His extensive research has uncovered a wealth of information regarding piracy attacks and the frequency and severity of the attacks by region, and it has assisted in developing strategies to deter or prevent the pirates from succeeding in their activities.

Mr. Gary Stubblefield retired after serving 20 years with the elite U.S. Navy SEAL Teams. During his career, he commanded SEAL Team THREE, a mobile sea base in the Persian Gulf, and retired after serving as the commodore for the entire Pacific fleet of the navy's special operations combatant craft. Mr. Stubblefield experienced combat in Vietnam, Central America, and the Persian Gulf. He has continued working in the commercial world in the development of small combatant craft and tactics. He has also spent a great deal of time over the past seven years working on commercial contracts dealing with the growing threat from modern-day pirates. He has recently sailed most of the high-threat piracy regions of the world on board his clients' vessels to help prevent or stop piracy activities against them.

For specific assistance, contact Vantage Systems Inc.:

TEL: 406-961-8451
E-Mail: stubbs@montana.com